Journey to Freedom®

MAYA ANGELOU

BY JUDITH E. HARPER

"LIFE IS PURE ADVENTURE, AND THE
SOONER WE REALIZE THAT, THE
QUICKER WE WILL BE ABLE TO TREAT
LIFE AS ART: TO BRING ALL OUR
ENERGIES TO EACH ENCOUNTER."

~ MAYA ANGELOU ~

Cover and page 4 caption: Maya Angelou attends a 2005 event honoring women in film.

Content Consultant: Neal A. Lester, PhD, Department of English, Arizona State University

Published in the United States of America by The Child's World®
1980 Lookout Drive, Mankato, MN 56003-1705
800-599-READ • www.childsworld.com

ACKNOWLEDGEMENTS

The Child's World®: Mary Berendes, Publishing Director

The Design Lab: Kathleen Petelinsek, Design; Gregory Lindholm, Page Production

Red Line Editorial: Amy Van Zee, Editorial Direction

PHOTOS

Cover and page 4: E. Neitzel/Getty Images

Interior: Clarence Hamm/AP Images, 5, 13; Russell Lee/Bettmann/Corbis, 7; Bettmann/Corbis, 8, 11, 17; AP Images, 9, 19, 21, 23; Getty Images, 10, 14; Hans Von Nolde/AP Images, 15; David Karp/AP Images, 18; G. Marshall Wilson/AP Images, 22; Mark Lennihan/AP Images, 24; Moneta Sleet Jr./AP Images, 26; Dan Nierling/AP Images, 27

LIBRARY OF CONGRESS CATALOGING-IN-PUBLICATION DATA

Harper, Judith E., 1953–

Maya Angelou / by Judith E. Harper.

  p. cm. — (Journey to freedom)

Includes bibliographical references and index.

ISBN 978-1-60253-131-4 (library bound : alk. paper)

1. Angelou, Maya—Juvenile literature. 2. African American authors—Biography—Juvenile literature. 3. African American women civil rights workers—Biography—Juvenile literature. I. Title. II. Series.

PS3551.N464Z693 2009

818'.5409—dc22

[B]

2009003651

CONTENTS

Maya Angelou worked on a San Francisco streetcar like this one when she was young.

Chapter One

FACING DISCRIMINATION

In 1943, Maya Angelou was a 15-year-old high school student in San Francisco, California. Her dream was to work as a conductor on the city's streetcars. She was deeply disappointed when her mother told her that the streetcar company would not accept Maya because she was black. Sure enough, when Maya went to the office of the Market Street Railway Company, the receptionist refused to give her an application. The receptionist also dodged Maya's questions about employment. Maya knew that this treatment was **discrimination**. She was not allowed to apply for the conductor job because of the color of her skin.

This encounter filled Maya with the courage to continue pursuing the conductor job.

She would not be turned away. Every day, she returned to the company office to sit and wait for an application. Three weeks later, the company finally granted her an interview. She was hired and became the first black person to work on the streetcars of San Francisco. Overflowing with pride, Maya was thrilled by her victory. She knew that she could achieve whatever she wanted most in life.

Maya Angelou is considered one of the greatest writers in the United States. Her books and poems are admired all over the world. She has also been a dancer, a singer, a songwriter, a playwright, a director, a producer, and a teacher. But Maya's life has not always been so successful. Many times, even when she tried her hardest, she met challenges. Each time, she found the strength to continue. When Maya talks to young people today, she tells them that they must keep on trying, even when experiences become difficult.

Maya Angelou was born Marguerite Annie Johnson in St. Louis, Missouri, on April 4, 1928. Her older brother, Bailey Johnson, was the first person to call her "Maya" when they were small children. In 1931, the family lived together in Long Beach, California. But that same year, when Maya was three years old, she and four-year-old Bailey said good-bye to their parents and their home. Together the children boarded a train for a cross-country journey—all on their own—to live with their grandmother in Stamps, Arkansas. Maya's parents

DRY GOODS AND GROCERIES

COL_E'S

PARKIN, ARK.

EEDS & SEEDS   Wt Empty 5800

A traveling grocery store in Arkansas in 1938

had recently divorced, and their mother realized she could not earn a living and care for her children at the same time. Maya and Bailey were bewildered by the move. Each child thought that they had done something terribly wrong to cause their mother to send them away.

Their grandmother, Momma Henderson, was a kind but strict woman. She took good care of Maya and Bailey. She was a deeply religious person and believed it was her duty to raise her grandchildren as devout Christians. Momma Henderson owned a general store in Stamps, a small country town. Although Momma Henderson had very little money, the family did not go hungry as many people did during the Great Depression of the 1930s.

The Great Depression was a time of economic hardship that lasted from late 1929 until the early 1940s. Many people lost their jobs and homes and depended on the government for food, housing, and jobs.

7

Like the rest of the southern United States at the time, the town of Stamps was **segregated**. Blacks lived in one section of town, and whites lived in another. Blacks could only attend black schools, buy food at black-only stores, and worship at black churches. If they were ill or dying, a white doctor would not treat them. If no black doctors or nurses were available, black people had to travel to another town to search for care or go without medical help.

Although there were exceptions, most white people in Stamps treated black people with very little respect. Some were cruel, and a few were violent

Children attending a segregated school in Virginia in 1947

toward black people. During Maya's childhood, the **lynching** of blacks by white mobs still occurred.

When Maya was very young, she seldom saw white people, so they did not seem real to her. She only saw them from afar and thought they looked like ghosts. As she grew older and came into contact with white people in Stamps, their unkindness toward her and her family angered her. Fortunately, the community of blacks in Stamps was strong. Maya's neighbors supported and cared for one another. The stories and humor they shared gave them the courage to face the **prejudice** and hatred they encountered daily.

Between 1882 and 1968, white mobs in the southern United States lynched more than 3,400 blacks.

A group in front of the White House in 1946 protests lynching.

A young actress in a 1979 movie about Maya Angelou's life

Chapter Two

STRUGGLING TO SURVIVE

hen Maya was seven years old, she made another long journey. This time, Maya and Bailey traveled to St. Louis, Missouri, to live with their mother. A year later, her mother's boyfriend **sexually abused** Maya when her mother was not home. The experience was **traumatic**. Terrified, Maya told no one because the man threatened to kill Bailey if she did. When her mother discovered the truth a few days later, she told the police, and the man was arrested. Maya gave her **testimony** at his trial, and the man was sentenced to jail. Shortly after he was released from jail, he was murdered. This frightened Maya. She believed that had she not spoken at the trial, the man would still be alive.

Maya convinced herself that her voice had played a part in killing the man. She vowed never to speak again.

As weeks passed, Maya's body healed, but her soul continued to suffer. Her determined silence disturbed Maya's mother. After several months, her mother gave up trying to break through the wall that Maya had built around herself. Her mother sent Maya and Bailey back to their grandmother in Arkansas. Momma Henderson and Bailey accepted and understood Maya's refusal to speak. Maya was grateful when Bailey tried to protect her from the hurtful comments of neighbors.

The period in which Maya was **mute** was a difficult one, but she learned a great deal from the experience. She kept her eyes wide open and carefully observed the world around her. She also lost herself in reading. Maya especially loved the poetry of William Shakespeare and Paul Laurence Dunbar.

About a year after Maya returned to Arkansas, Bertha Flowers, the most educated black woman

Paul Laurence Dunbar was one of the first black American poets to become famous nationwide. He wrote about black heroes and the good qualities of black people. He was born in Dayton, Ohio, in 1872.

Maya Angelou admired poet Paul Laurence Dunbar.

11

in Stamps, invited Maya to her home. Maya was thrilled that this special woman had noticed her. Flowers read poetry to Maya and told her about the beauty of the human voice. Maya borrowed a book of poetry from her and agreed to choose a passage to recite at their next visit. Maya felt special. Through her friendship with Flowers, Maya began to believe in herself. Eventually, she started to speak again.

Maya was an excellent student through her young school years. She graduated from the eighth grade at the top of her class. Momma noticed that Maya and Bailey were growing up quickly—Maya was 13 and Bailey was 14. Momma told them that she was becoming too old to care for them, and it was time that they live with their mother, who was living in San Francisco, California. Momma never said so, but Maya believed that she was concerned about her grandchildren's future. Momma knew that they would have more opportunities and freedom in California than they had in the segregated South. Maya and Bailey moved to San Francisco.

Maya was an achiever in high school as well. She enjoyed dance and acting classes. She won a **scholarship** to the California Labor School.

In 1945, soon after she graduated from high school, Maya gave birth to a son, Clyde Bailey Johnson. She was 17 years old. She did not know the baby's father well, and she did not want to marry him. When Maya's mother offered her the chance to live at home with her

Bertha Flowers was a true friend to young Maya. After spending time with Flowers, Maya began keeping a scrapbook journal to record her thoughts about her experiences and about the books she read.

baby and attend college, Maya experienced a sudden surge of independence. Although she very much wanted to go to college, she felt an even stronger need to be on her own. She wanted to prove to herself and to her family that she could support herself and her baby, so she rented a room and found a job as a cook.

Maya Angelou was determined to be independent when she lived in San Francisco.

Chapter Three

A DIFFICULT ROAD TO SUCCESS

he next few years were a constant struggle for Maya. She worked as a cook and a waitress. She searched for good childcare for baby Clyde. She moved from place to place and discovered how difficult life was for a single mother.

For a brief time, Maya experimented with drugs. Soon a close friend, Troubadour Martin, shocked Maya into stopping her drug use. Martin explained to her how drugs were controlling and destroying his life. Maya would never forget the lesson, and she has always been grateful for it.

Maya realized she needed more support from her friends and family. She moved back in with her mother in San Francisco and found satisfying work in a music store. Not long after, Maya married another music lover, Tosh Angelos, a Greek American. But after two years of marriage, they divorced.

Maya was inspired to reach for her lifelong goal of becoming a performer. When Maya was in her mid-twenties, the managers of The Purple Onion nightclub hired her as a calypso singer and dancer. She began to use the name Maya Angelou. Her act was a success. After **talent scouts** watched her perform, she was offered a role in an upcoming Broadway show.

On the same day Angelou received this good news, she was also asked to be a leading dancer in a traveling company of artists. They were performing *Porgy and Bess,* a popular American opera. Angelou was thrilled to be offered two roles. She had no trouble deciding which part to accept. She had always wanted to travel and to be a member of an all-black theatrical company. In 1954, she joined the cast of *Porgy and Bess.*

Maya Angelou chose her last name by slightly changing the last name of her first husband, Tosh Angelos.

Actors Leontyne Price and William Warfield in a scene from *Porgy and Bess*

George Gershwin composed Porgy and Bess. *It tells the love story of a black man and woman. It became a very popular American opera.*

With this success came some pain. *Porgy and Bess* toured many nations in Europe, the Middle East, and Latin America. Angelou was unable to take her son with her during these travels. Angelou felt terrible leaving her 9-year-old child at home with her mother. The separation was difficult for both Angelou and her son. When Angelou returned home many months later, she promised herself that she would not be separated from Guy (Clyde's new nickname for himself) again.

In 1959, when Guy was 14, mother and son moved to New York City. Angelou became involved in a community in the part of the city called Harlem. She knew she wanted to work as a writer. Angelou joined the Harlem Writers Guild, a group of hard-working black writers.

One day it was Angelou's turn to read what she had written to the other guild members. When she finished reading her play, one writer named John Clarke harshly criticized it. Angelou was devastated and thought of giving up on writing. However, Clarke spoke to Angelou again. He explained that talent is not enough to become a writer. He told her that she would need to work hard and rewrite her stories many times. Angelou listened. She knew she had a difficult road ahead of her if she wanted to be a writer. She promised herself she would not quit.

James Baldwin was another writer who encouraged Angelou and became her friend.

Maya Angelou (right) with
Coretta Scott King, widow of
Martin Luther King Jr., in 1997

Chapter Four

THE CIVIL RIGHTS MOVEMENT

n the late 1950s, Harlem was a place of great action and change. Blacks were protesting racial discrimination and prejudice. They were also joining **civil rights** workers who opposed racial segregation in the South. It thrilled Angelou to watch the **civil rights movement** gain strength and power. Like many blacks, Angelou believed that racial equality was no longer an impossible dream, but rather a reality within reach.

After hearing civil rights leader Martin Luther King Jr. speak, Angelou was determined to join his cause through his group, the Southern Christian Leadership Conference (SCLC).

With her friend Godfrey Cambridge, Angelou gathered black performers to appear in *Cabaret for Freedom*. She created the production to raise money for the SCLC. It was enormously successful and also raised awareness about the civil rights struggle.

After this victory, Angelou worked briefly as a northern coordinator of the SCLC in 1960. During this exciting time, Angelou met Vusumzi Make, a freedom fighter from South Africa. Make was traveling the world to gain support for his people's fight against **apartheid**. Angelou fell in love with Make and admired his fight to help his people. After a very brief courtship, they agreed to consider their relationship a true marriage, although they never married legally.

Apartheid was the legal policy in South Africa that separated blacks from whites in all public places. In 1991, the South African government removed the last apartheid laws.

A group of South Africans protests apartheid in 1960.

THE CIVIL RIGHTS MOVEMENT

Angelou and Guy moved with Make to Cairo, Egypt. While in Cairo, Angelou became worried about the family's finances and was bored with her role as a housewife. Though Make did not want her to work, Angelou pursued a job as an editor at the *Arab Observer,* an English-language newspaper. Make was enraged when he found out. Angelou knew that she needed to be independent. In 1962, she separated from Make and moved with Guy to the city of Accra, Ghana.

Ghana was an exciting, colorful, newly independent nation in West Africa. Angelou began working and teaching at the University of Ghana, where Guy was a student. She also improved her writing skills by submitting articles to newspapers.

While in Ghana, Angelou once again met black leader Malcolm X. Years before, she had heard him speak in Harlem and had talked with him about her civil rights activities. Malcolm X had opposed Dr. King's strategy of nonviolence—the use of peaceful, rather than violent, methods to achieve civil rights. Malcolm X had preached a more radical message of freedom at any cost. Angelou had admired Malcolm X but did not agree with all of his ideas.

In Ghana, Angelou discovered that Malcolm X had changed. He had decided that he must work with white and black leaders all over the world to achieve civil rights in the United States and independence for blacks in Africa. Malcolm X hoped to convince African leaders to pressure the United States to give blacks more civil rights.

When Malcolm X first became a prominent leader, he believed that blacks would be better off living separately from whites. He thought that this was the only way they would be able to achieve equality.

Malcolm X in New York in 1964

Angelou was inspired to help Malcolm X with his new mission, the Organization of Afro-American Unity (OAAU). He formed this group so that Africans, African Americans, and all people of African **ancestry** could work together to achieve human rights throughout the world. He hired Angelou to serve as a coordinator of the OAAU. She was to begin this new job as soon as she returned to the United States. But Malcolm X was **assassinated** on February 21, 1965, just a few days after Angelou arrived in the United States. She was in anguish over Malcolm X's death. She grieved for him and for their cause. After the assassination, Angelou continued to support the civil rights movement. But she also decided that she would no longer play such an active role.

Maya Angelou pictured around 1970

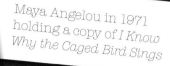

Chapter Five

FULFILLMENT

I n the late 1960s, Angelou focused her energies on her writing. In 1970, her book *I Know Why the Caged Bird Sings* was published. This first volume of her autobiography told the story of her childhood. It became an immediate best seller and was nominated for the National Book Award, a very high honor.

During the 1970s and 1980s, Angelou worked intently and became more successful as an author. She wrote and published more volumes of her autobiography and several books of poetry. In 1972, she was nominated for a Pulitzer Prize for her first published book of verse, *Just Give Me a Cool Drink of Water 'fore I Diiie*. When Angelou

Written by Alex Haley, Roots *tells the story of a black family's journey from slavery to freedom. Angelou was nominated for an Emmy Award for her performance.*

wrote the script for the movie *Georgia, Georgia* in 1972, she became the first black woman to have a screenplay produced in Hollywood. In 1977, she appeared in the popular television miniseries, *Roots.* In 1981, Angelou was named the Reynolds Professor of American Studies at Wake Forest University in Winston-Salem, North Carolina. She continues to work and live there today, as well as in Harlem.

Maya Angelou reading her poem at President Bill Clinton's inauguration in 1993

When President Bill Clinton planned his 1993 inauguration, he invited Angelou to compose and recite a special poem for the ceremony. She was deeply honored. By the time she finished the poem, she had written more than 200 pages. She edited the poem down to a shorter length, yet it was still powerful. On January 20, 1993, Angelou read "On the Pulse of Morning" to millions of Americans.

Angelou is still passionate about writing. When she writes, she allows no distractions. She starts working early in the morning. When she finishes writing, she spends more time editing her work. Angelou admits that even though she must overcome her fear of writing every single day, it is the most important and fulfilling part of her life.

Angelou feels a special closeness to children. In December of 1996, she was appointed as a National Ambassador for the United Nations International Children's Emergency Fund (UNICEF). In this role, she makes Americans aware of the importance of UNICEF's work. She also helps raise money to aid children in need around the world.

Because reading helped Angelou survive her childhood, she also spreads the message that books are valuable. Angelou has written many children's books. She believes that reading empowers children to work toward their most treasured goals. She also hopes that her work as an activist will help to eliminate **illiteracy**.

When Angelou writes, she likes to have a thesaurus and a dictionary next to her. She also keeps a deck of cards nearby for an occasional game of solitaire.

Maya Angelou won a Grammy Award in 1994.

Angelou is also an accomplished **orator**. With nearly every speech, she finds a way to tell people that courage is the human quality she admires most. She also wants people to understand what she means by courage. To Angelou, courage means being afraid but facing those fears. Angelou has won three Grammy Awards for her spoken-word albums.

Maya Angelou has spent a lifetime facing her fears, pushing through them, rising above them, and never giving up. Although she has had many successes, she admits that her challenges have also been useful because they made her stronger. Thanks to Angelou's courage, she has been strong enough to help other people through the power and lessons of her stories and poetry.

Maya Angelou gives a powerful speech at the University of Northern Iowa in 2000.

TIME LINE

1928
Marguerite Annie Johnson is born in St. Louis, Missouri, on April 4.

1943
Maya becomes the first black streetcar conductor in San Francisco.

1945
Maya graduates from high school in San Francisco and gives birth to her son, Clyde Bailey "Guy" Johnson.

1953
Maya lands a job singing and dancing at The Purple Onion, a San Francisco nightclub. She begins to go by the name Maya Angelou.

1954
Angelou joins the cast of *Porgy and Bess* and travels to nations in Europe, the Middle East, and Latin America.

1959
Angelou moves to New York City with her son and joins the Harlem Writers Guild.

1960

Angelou meets Martin Luther King Jr. and Malcolm X. She forms a close relationship with Vusumzi Make, a South African freedom fighter.

1960

Angelou moves to Cairo, Egypt, with Vusumzi Make and her son.

1962

Angelou and her son move to Accra, Ghana.

1965

Angelou returns to the United States and learns of the assassination of Malcolm X.

1970

I Know Why the Caged Bird Sings is published.

1972

Angelou becomes the first black woman to have a screenplay produced in Hollywood.

1977

Angelou is nominated for an Emmy Award for her performance in the television miniseries *Roots*.

1993

Angelou recites one of her poems at President Bill Clinton's inauguration.

1996

UNICEF appoints Angelou as a National Ambassador.

2002

The sixth and final volume of Angelou's autobiography, *A Song Flung Up to Heaven*, is published.

GLOSSARY

ancestry
(an-sess-tree)
Ancestry is the line of family members who lived before a person. Angelou joined Malcolm X to help all people of African ancestry have equality.

apartheid
(uh-part-hate)
Apartheid is the former policy of the South African government of separating blacks and whites. Angelou fell in love with a freedom fighter who protested apartheid.

assassinated
(uh-sass-uh-nay-ted)
When an important or well-known person is assassinated, he or she is murdered. Malcolm X was assassinated in 1965.

calypso
(kuh-lip-soh)
Calypso is a type of music from the West Indies with a lively rhythm and beat. Angelou performed as a calypso singer and dancer.

civil rights
(siv-il rites)
Civil rights are personal freedoms that belong to all U.S. citizens. Angelou joined with civil rights workers to fight for black equality.

civil rights movement
(siv-il rites moov-munt)
The civil rights movement is the name given to the struggle for equal rights for blacks in the United States during the 1950s and 1960s. Angelou took part in the civil rights movement.

discrimination
(diss-krim-i-nay-shun)
Discrimination is the unfair treatment of people based on differences of race, gender, religion, or culture. Angelou experienced discrimination when she was not allowed to apply for a job on a San Francisco streetcar.

illiteracy
(il-lit-ur-a-see)
Illiteracy is the inability to read and write. Angelou works to eliminate illiteracy.

lynching
(linch-ing)
Lynching is putting a person to death, usually by hanging, without legal cause. When Angelou was growing up, lynching was common in the South.

mute
(myoot)
To be mute is to not speak. After she was sexually abused, Angelou was voluntarily mute.

orator
(or-eh-ter)
An orator is a person who is very good at speaking to the public. Angelou is an excellent orator.

prejudice
(prej-uh-diss)
Prejudice is a negative feeling or opinion about someone without just cause. Angelou faced instances of prejudice throughout her life.

scholarship
(skahl-ur-ship)
A scholarship is an award of money given to a high-achieving student to be used toward his or her education. Angelou received a scholarship to attend the California Labor School.

segregated
(seg-ruh-gay-tud)
When something is segregated, racial, class, gender, or ethnic groups are kept apart. When Angelou was young, society in the South was segregated.

sexually abused
(sek-shuh-wa-lee uh-byoozd)
To be sexually abused is to be forced into unwanted sexual activity. Angelou was sexually abused by her mother's boyfriend when she was eight years old.

talent scouts
(tal-unt skowts)
Talent scouts are people who find other people for a special activity. Talent scouts offered Angelou a role in a Broadway play after watching her perform.

testimony
(tess-tuh-moh-nee)
A testimony is a statement a witness gives in court. Angelou gave her testimony after she was sexually abused.

traumatic
(traw-mat-ik)
When something is traumatic, it is upsetting and painful. Angelou had a traumatic experience when she was sexually abused as a child.

FURTHER INFORMATION

Books

Kite, L. Patricia. *Maya Angelou.* Minneapolis, MN: Lerner, 2006.

Landau, Elaine. *The Civil Rights Movement in America.* New York: Children's Press, 2007.

Mangrum, Allison. *African American Writers Who Inspired Change.* Brea, CA: Ballard & Tighe, 2006.

Wilson, Edwin Graves, ed. *Poetry for Young People: Maya Angelou.* New York: Sterling, 2007.

Videos

ABC News Classics: Maya Angelou. ABC, 2007.

Black History: Contributions to Society in the Arts, Sports, Science, and More. St. Clair Vision, 2007.

Web Sites

Visit our Web page for links about Maya Angelou:

http://www.childsworld.com/links

NOTE TO PARENTS, TEACHERS, AND LIBRARIANS: We routinely verify our Web links to make sure they are safe, active sites—so encourage your readers to check them out!

INDEX